Why Is It So Hard to Go Back to the Moon?

By Mark R. Whittington

For Steph, who departed beyond the final frontier of death far too soon.

Acknowledgements: The number of people who were helpful in the production of this long essay are too numerous to mention. But I would like to take special note of the help Dr. Karina Stokes rendered as well as my wife Chantal, my forever first reader and best critic, without which the work would not have been possible.

That's One Small Step for Man. One Giant Leap for Mankind

Everyone who was of age on July 20, 1969, remembers where they were when men landed on the Moon. I was on a family vacation in Panama City Beach, Florida on that day. My family, along with another family with whom we had been friendly for years, crowed into a single beach-side motel room with one of the only working TVs to watch the first moonwalk.

The TV was ancient even for that era, a tiny black and white that could only get one channel. The quality of television transmission would have been considered laughable by modern standards. But, as anyone who has seen that wonderful Australian movie *The Dish* knows, the technological achievement of getting television pictures from the surface of the Moon to TV screens on Earth was as impressive, in its own way, as getting men there and back.

The images that traveled from the Moon to millions of television sets on Earth were in black and white and fuzzy to boot. But the reason they were more beautiful than any special effects-laden science fiction movie was that they were real. This was not some cinematographer's conception of what a voyage to the Moon would be like. It was a voyage to the Moon.

Neil Armstrong was a blindingly white figure on the television screen as he descended down the ladder from the lunar module hatch to the ground. He lingered on the bottom of the ladder for tantalizing minutes as he observed the condition of the LM's landing pads. Then, the moment arrived when he said, "I'm going to step off the LM now."

A billion people on a planet that contained only a little more than three billion people held their collective breaths.

"That's one small step for man. One giant leap for mankind."

History is often bifurcated by singular events that change everything. So it was with the first Apollo moon landing. Before, the moon was terra incognita, a bright disk in the sky filled with mystery and wonder. After, it was a place where men had walked and explored, bringing back rocks and soil for generations of scientists to study, as valuable in their own way as the gold which the Spanish conquistadors had sought.

The rest of the two-hour excursion passed as if were a dream. Buzz Aldrin soon joined Armstrong on the lunar surface. They unveiled a plaque that commemorated the event. "Here men from the planet Earth first set foot upon the Moon. July 1969, A.D. We came in peace for all mankind." Later, they erected the American flag to note the fact that those men were Americans, their mission supported and paid for by the United States. In the middle of their collecting rocks and setting up experiments, Armstrong and Aldrin took a call from President Richard Nixon.

Then, in the fullness of time, the two men took their geology treasure back into the lunar module and blasted off for a rendezvous and docking with the Apollo command module then in lunar orbit.

The Apollo Moon landing was so successful and, dare I say, so cool, that we did it five more times with missions of increasing scope and sophistication. As a bonus, the world looked on with anxiousness as the crew of Apollo 13 fought to come home after an explosion in the service module. The epic voyage became one of the greatest movies about space travel in history, directed by Ron Howard and starring Tom Hanks.

Then, after the last Apollo moon mission departed the lunar surface in December 1972, we stopped.

Why the United States stopped going to the Moon, even with the spacecraft already built for three more missions, is something of a mystery for those who came of age after the end of the First Age of Lunar Exploration. Logically, the United States should have built on the knowledge and experience it had won during the Apollo missions to the Moon to continue to conduct lunar expeditions, building up to a permanent lunar base.

Why the United States turned away from the Moon, just when it had achieved it, is part of the subject of this small book. I will also try to explain why two attempts to revive a lunar program crashed on the rocks of politics. I will also try to lay out a political strategy for making a third attempt to return to the Moon, this time successfully.

Most people can recite from memory the first words spoken on the moon. But few people remember the last words, at least officially, said by Apollo 17 astronaut Gene Cernan.[1]

---

[1] "These Were the Last Words that were Said on the Moon" Eric Limer, Gizmodo, 12/15/2012.

"I'm on the surface; and, as I take man's last step from the surface, back home for some time to come - but we believe not too long into the future - I'd like to just [say] what I believe history will record. That America's challenge of today has forged man's destiny of tomorrow. And, as we leave the Moon at Taurus-Littrow, we leave as we came and, God willing, as we shall return: with peace and hope for all mankind. Godspeed the crew of Apollo 17."

The second-to-last sentence contains a promise that has yet to be fulfilled. That fact is a blot on our civilization that will only be wiped out when the next moonboots hit the ground on the other side of the airless sea.

The Life and Premature Death of the Apollo Program

When President John F. Kennedy made his remarks before
a joint session of Congress on May 25, 1961, the American
space program was in a bad way. Having been beaten by
the Soviets in the race to put the first satellite into low
Earth orbit, the United States had been beaten again when
Yuri Gagarin became the first man to orbit the Earth on
April 12, 1961.

Clearly, something had to be done.

Just over a week later, President Kennedy sent a memo to
the office of Vice-President Lyndon Johnson and asked him
the following questions in his capacity as chairman of the
White House space council.

> 1. Do we have a chance of beating the
> Soviets by putting a laboratory in space, or
> by a trip around the moon, or by a rocket to
> go to the moon and back with a man? Is
> there any other space program which
> promises dramatic results in which we could
> win?
>
> 2. How much additional would it cost?
>
> 3. Are we working 24 hours a day on
> existing programs? If not, why not? If not,
> will you make recommendations to me as to
> how work can be speeded up?
>
> 4. In building large boosters should we put
> our emphasis on nuclear, chemical, or liquid

fuel, or a combination of these three?

5. Are we making maximum effort? Are we achieving necessary results?"[2]

Eight days later Johnson responded. Noting that space achievements increasingly were being seen as an indicator of world leadership and that if the United States did not increase its efforts, it would in due course become hopelessly behind the Soviets, Johnson recommended the moon race.[3]

It was with this evaluation in mind that President Kennedy called a joint session of Congress on May 25. The speech, which was about "urgent national needs," contained a laundry list of proposals. All most people remember was the following:

"First, I believe that this nation should commit itself to achieving the goal, before this decade is out, of landing a man on the moon and returning him safely to the Earth. No single space project in this period will be more impressive to mankind, or more important for the long-range exploration of space; and none will be so difficult or expensive to accomplish. We propose to accelerate the development of the appropriate lunar space craft. We propose to develop alternate liquid and solid fuel boosters, much larger than any now being developed, until certain which is superior. We propose additional funds for other engine development and for unmanned explorations-- explorations which are particularly important for one purpose which this nation will never overlook: the survival

[2] John F. Kennedy, Memorandum for the Vice President, 04/12/1961.
[3] Lyndon B. Johnson, Memorandum for the President, "Evaluation of Space Program." 04/28/1961.

of the man who first makes this daring flight. But in a very real sense, it will not be one man going to the moon--if we make this judgment affirmatively, it will be an entire nation. For all of us must work to put him there."[4]

The Apollo program was motivated by the Cold War between the United States and its allies and the Soviet Union. At its core, it was a psychological warfare strategy to prove the superiority of western democracy over Soviet communism. It was the ultimate shock and awe campaign, but without bombing or gunfire. Apollo could only be compared to the Panama Canal or the Manhattan Project in its scope and its vision.

Kennedy repeated his call for landing a man on the moon during a speech made at Rice University in Houston, Texas, on September 12, 1962. He repeated the themes of the Cold War competition with the Soviets, adding references to America's pioneering past to support the moon landing effort.

> We set sail on this new sea because there is new knowledge to be gained, and new rights to be won, and they must be won and used for the progress of all people. For space science, like nuclear science and all technology, has no conscience of its own. Whether it will become a force for good or ill depends on man, and only if the United States occupies a position of pre-eminence can we help decide whether this new ocean will be a sea of peace or a new terrifying theater of war. I do not say the we should or

---

[4] JFK's Moonshot speech to Congress, 5/25/1961.

will go unprotected against the hostile misuse of space any more than we go unprotected against the hostile use of land or sea, but I do say that space can be explored and mastered without feeding the fires of war, without repeating the mistakes that man has made in extending his writ around this globe of ours.

There is no strife, no prejudice, no national conflict in outer space as yet. Its hazards are hostile to us all. Its conquest deserves the best of all mankind, and its opportunity for peaceful cooperation many never come again. But why, some say, the Moon? Why choose this as our goal? And they may well ask, why climb the highest mountain? Why, 35 years ago, fly the Atlantic? Why does Rice play Texas?

We choose to go to the Moon. We choose to go to the Moon in this decade and do the other things, not because they are easy, but because they are hard, because that goal will serve to organize and measure the best of our energies and skills, because that challenge is one that we are willing to accept, one we are unwilling to postpone, and one which we intend to win, and the others, too.

"It is for these reasons that I regard the decision last year to shift our efforts in space from low to high gear as among the most important decisions that will be made during

my incumbency in the office of the
Presidency.[5]

Nevertheless, about a year later, Kennedy seemed to shy
away from the idea of a race to the Moon as a means of
super-power competition. He made a surprise speech before
the UN General Assembly on September 20, 1963, in
which he held out the idea of a joint America/Soviet lunar
expedition. [6]

The proposal was made for two reasons. First, not only
Kennedy but Congress was starting to get leery about the
enormous costs of the Apollo program. Sharing resources
with the Soviets would seem to be a good way to share the
burden. Second, by late 1963, Kennedy was looking for
ways to establish friendlier relations with the Soviet Union.
A joint space mission seemed to fit right into that strategy.

The joint moon mission proposal went nowhere. The
Soviets were cool about the idea. Congress and the
American public were decidedly hostile. It smacked of
changing directions in midstream. It was understood that
the Apollo program was meant to beat the Soviets, not to
make friends of them. In any case, the idea died with
Kennedy when he was assassinated in Dallas. Though
President Johnson tried to revive it briefly, Congress made
sure through legislation that it would never fly.

---

[5] John F. Kennedy Moon Speech, Rice Stadium. 9/12/1962.
[6] The Kennedy Proposal for a Joint Moon Flight, Chicago Tribune,
1963.

It turned out that President Kennedy was not the only one who was starting to get sticker shock concerning the Apollo program. Both the House and the Senate proposed deep cuts in NASA funding for FY1964, essentially proposing a $5.1 billion budget that would have placed the goal of landing on the Moon by the end of the decade in doubt. [7]

Sen. William Proxmire, a Democrat from Wisconsin, was a driving force behind this effort, proposing an amendment in the Senate that cut NASA funding roughly $700 million below the Kennedy administration's request. Proxmire was later to become a tireless foe of manned space flight, opposing virtually every NASA program that involved astronauts, including the space shuttle and the Space Station Freedom programs. He also opposed government funding for SETI, the Search for Extra-Terrestrial Intelligence.

Ironically, opposition to the Apollo program also died with President Kennedy. Apollo became a memorial to the fallen president, a sentiment that sustained the program for the next nine years, until the last moon landing to date, the Apollo 17 mission in December of 1972. Many historians give short shrift to the moon landing goal, but Kennedy himself believed that it was the most important decision of his administration. It will almost certainly be the one remembered most, long after the Cuban Missile Crisis, the nuclear test ban treaty, and the civil rights struggle are consigned to history.

The Apollo 11 moon landing was one of the singular events in human history, watched by upwards of a billion people

---

[7] John F. Kennedy and the Race to the Moon, Palgrave Macmillan John Logsdon, 2013

in real time on live TV and radio broadcasts. This viewership was on a planet that had 3.5 or so billion people at the time. The moon landing garnered for the United States a considerable amount of international prestige, something that was somewhat tattered by the Vietnam War and civil strife.

Even so, the American people, at least according to polling data gathered by historian Roger Launius, were at best tepid in their response to the Apollo moon landing.[8] Only during the flight of Apollo 11 did more than 50 percent of the American people support the proposition that the moon landings were worth the cost. This was one reason that the politicians in Washington were disposed to pull back on space spending, even going so far as cancelling the last three moon landing missions, despite the fact that the hardware had already been built and that savings were minimal.

The Apollo 11 launch was actually the venue of a protest march, led by a civil rights leader named Rev. Ralph Abernathy.[9] Several hundred people showed up at Cape Canaveral to protest what they saw as misplaced priorities, spending money on expeditions to the moon instead of feeding the poor. He was met by then-NASA Administrator, Thomas Paine, who argued that the great advances made in the exploration of space were child's play compared to the intractable problems of poverty. Paine said, "If we could solve the problems of poverty by not pushing the button to launch men to the Moon tomorrow,

---

[8] Public opinion polls and perceptions of US human spaceflight, Roger D Launius, Space Policy July 19, 2003.
[9] The Apollo 11 Mission and the Challenge of Solving the Plight of the Poor, Roger Launius Blog, 6/6/2014.

then we would not push that button." The implication clearly was that stopping the lunar expedition would not solve the problems of poverty. Nevertheless, Abernathy's position gained some resonance in the minds of many Americans, particularly politicians on the left.

There is some evidence that the Apollo moon landing program was of net economic benefit for the United States, something that is unique for a government program. According to Jerome Schnee, of the Business Administration Department at Rutgers University, [10]at least three economic studies conducted in the 1970s and 1980s suggested that research and development derived from the space program was of net economic benefit for the United States. Much of this occurred in the form of technological spin-offs, technology developed for flying to the moon that wound up having more earthly applications. While NASA and some space enthusiasts have tended to oversell this phenomenon, it still exists and should be taken into account when considering the cost/benefit equation for government space spending.

Some libertarian analysts suggest that the spinoff argument is folly, that money spent on space could more efficiently be spent in the private sector. This may or may not be so, but it tends to ignore unpleasant political realities. If NASA were abolished, and all government space programs were scrapped, there is little hope that the money saved would be plowed into the private sector. It would likely be spent on other government programs, such as social welfare, which would produce far less benefit for the United States.

---

[10] The Economic Impacts of the U.S. Space Program, Jerome Schnee, Business Administration Department, Rutgers University. 1980

The Apollo program did lead to a certain degree of good will for the United States around the world. Roger Launius suggests that the Apollo moon landing "met with an ecstatic reaction around the globe, as everyone shared in the success of the astronauts. The front pages of newspapers everywhere suggested how strong the enthusiasm was. NASA estimated that because of nearly worldwide radio and television coverage, more than half the population of the planet was aware of the events of Apollo 11."[11]

Paul Spudis, a lunar geologist who writes frequently about space policy, suggests that it had a different reaction among the Soviet leadership, one that reverberated to the very end of the Cold War, affecting perceptions of another big, technological project. "President Kennedy started Apollo and the race to the Moon as a Cold War gambit; a way to demonstrate the superiority of a free and democratic way of life to that of our communist adversaries. That goal was successfully achieved to a degree still not fully appreciated today. The success of the Apollo program gave America something it did not realize was so important – technical credibility. When President Reagan announced SDI twenty years later, the Soviets were against it, not because it was destabilizing and provocative, but because they thought we would succeed, rendering their vast military machine, assembled at great cost to their people and economy, obsolete in an instant. Among other factors, this hastened the end of the Cold War in our favor."[12]

---

[11] Apollo 11 and the World, Roger Launius, Smithsonian Air and Space Magazine, 7/15/2009.
[12] Apollo: An American Victory in the Cold War, Paul Spudis, Spudis Lunar Resources, July, 1999.

In other words, the Soviets concluded that if the Americans could land a man on the moon, they could succeed in President Reagan's goal in making nuclear weapons obsolete with a space-based missile defense system. Spudis draws a direct line from the Apollo program to SDI and, by implication, to the American victory in the Cold War. The analysis makes one think how much sooner the Cold War could have been won had America doubled down on Apollo and driven the lesson of American technological superiority home more keenly.

The scientific returns from Apollo are almost beyond evaluation. Smithsonian's Air and Space Magazine lists just ten of many discoveries that reveal much about the Moon's geology and history. Those were:

1. **The Moon is not a primordial object; it is an evolved terrestrial planet with internal zoning similar to that of Earth.**

   Before Apollo, the state of the Moon was a subject of almost unlimited speculation. We now know that the Moon is made of rocky material that has been variously melted, erupted through volcanoes, and crushed by meteorite impacts. The Moon possesses a thick crust (60 km), a fairly uniform lithosphere (60-1000 km), and a partly liquid asthenosphere (1000-1740 km); a small iron core at the bottom of the asthenosphere is possible but unconfirmed. Some rocks give hints for ancient magnetic fields although no planetary field exists today.

2. **The Moon is ancient and still preserves an early history (the first billion years) that must be common to all terrestrial planets.**

The extensive record of meteorite craters on the Moon, when calibrated using absolute ages of rock samples, provides a key for unravelling time scales for the geologic evolution of Mercury, Venus, and Mars based on their individual crater records. Photogeologic interpretation of other planets is based largely on lessons learned from the Moon. Before Apollo, however, the origin of lunar impact craters was not fully understood and the origin of similar craters on Earth was highly debated.

3. **The youngest Moon rocks are virtually as old as the oldest Earth rocks. The earliest processes and events that probably affected both planetary bodies can now only be found on the Moon.**

Moon rock ages range from about 3.2 billion years in the maria (dark, low basins) to nearly 4.6 billion years in the terrae (light, rugged highlands). Active geologic forces, including plate tectonics and erosion, continuously repave the oldest surfaces on Earth whereas old surfaces persist with little disturbance on the Moon.

4. **The Moon and Earth are genetically related and formed from different proportions of a common reservoir of materials.**

The distinctively similar oxygen isotopic compositions of Moon rocks and Earth rocks clearly show common ancestry. Relative to Earth, however, the Moon was highly depleted in iron and in volatile elements that are needed to form atmospheric gases and water.

5. **The Moon is lifeless; it contains no living organisms, fossils, or native organic compounds.**

Extensive testing revealed no evidence for life, past or present, among the lunar samples. Even non-biological organic compounds are amazingly absent; traces can be attributed to contamination by meteorites.

6. **All Moon rocks originated through high-temperature processes with little or no involvement with water. They are roughly divisible into three types: basalts, anorthosites, and breccias.**

Basalts are dark lava rocks that fill mare basins; they generally resemble, but are much older than, lavas that comprise the oceanic crust of Earth. Anorthosites are light rocks that form the ancient highlands; they generally resemble, but are much older than, the most ancient rocks on Earth. Breccias are composite rocks formed from all other rock types through crushing, mixing, and sintering during meteorite impacts. The Moon has no sandstones, shales, or limestones such as testify to the importance of water-borne processes on Earth.

7. **Early in its history, the Moon was melted to great depths to form a "magma ocean." The lunar highlands contain the remnants of early, low density rocks that floated to the surface of the magma ocean.**

The lunar highlands were formed about 4.4-4.6 billion years ago by flotation of an early, feldspar-rich crust on a magma ocean that covered the Moon to a depth of many tens of kilometers or more. Innumerable meteorite impacts through geologic time reduced much of the ancient crust to arcuate mountain ranges between basins.

8. **The lunar magma ocean was followed by a series of huge asteroid impacts that created basins which were later filled by lava flows.**

The large, dark basins such as Mare Imbrium are gigantic impact craters, formed early in lunar history, that were later filled by lava flows about 3.2-3.9 billion years ago. Lunar volcanism occurred mostly as lava floods that spread horizontally; volcanic fire fountains produced deposits of orange and emerald-green glass beads.

9. **The Moon is slightly asymmetrical in bulk form, possibly as a consequence of its evolution under Earth's gravitational influence. Its crust is thicker on the far side, while most volcanic basins — and unusual mass concentrations — occur on the near side.**

Mass is not distributed uniformly inside the Moon. Large mass concentrations ("Mascons") lie beneath the surface of many large lunar basins and probably represent thick accumulations of dense lava. Relative to its geometric center, the Moon's center of mass is displaced toward Earth by several kilometers.

---

10. **The surface of the Moon is covered by a rubble pile of rock fragments and dust, called the lunar regolith, that contains a unique radiation history of the Sun which is of importance to understanding climate changes on Earth.**

The regolith was produced by innumerable meteorite impacts through geologic time. Surface rocks and mineral grains are distinctively enriched in chemical elements and isotopes implanted by solar radiation. As such, the Moon has recorded four billion years of the Sun's history to a degree of completeness that we are unlikely to find elsewhere. [13]

---

[13] Top Ten Scientific Discoveries Made During Apollo Exploration of the Moon, Smithsonian Air and Space Magazine

Using analytical tools that did not exist during the Apollo lunar missions, scientists continue to make new expansions in knowledge.

The closing question for this chapter is, was the Apollo program, which cost roughly $100 billion in current dollars, worth it? It seems that by every measure, politically, economically, and scientifically, the answer has to be yes. But that did not matter to those who saw large-scale space adventures as an affront to their political priorities.

The Space Task Group

When Richard Nixon assumed the presidency, one of the questions he faced was what to do with the space program he had inherited. To study that question, he established a Space Task Group, which was headed by Vice-President Agnew, in February, 1969. The mandate for the group was to develop some options for a post-Apollo space program to which President Nixon could affix his name, much as President Kennedy had done with the Apollo moon landing program.

In September, 1969, the Space Task Group presented its recommendations.[14] They offered three scenarios based on different levels of funding. The major differences in the three funding levels concerned the year in which a Mars expedition would take place. In the first scenario, in which NASA funding would rise to between $8 and $10 billion (in 1969 dollars) per year by 1980, people would have departed to Mars in 1981. In the second scenario, spending would peak at $8 billion in the early 1980s, and the Mars expedition would take place in 1986. The third scenario would defer the Mars expedition indefinitely. While there was some verbiage about continuing and even expanding the Apollo program and its associated Apollo Applications Project, the third option would have concentrated on building a space station and a reusable space shuttle.

President Nixon did not comment on the report until March 7, 1970, when he appeared to regard the recommendations of the report favorably, but was somewhat vague about how his administration would respond to them. He outlined six objectives for the space program going forward:

---

[14] Report of the Space Task Group, NASA History Archives, 1969.

1. We should continue to explore the Moon. Future Apollo manned lunar landings will be spaced so as to maximize our scientific return from each mission, always providing, of course, for the safety of those who undertake these ventures. Our decisions about manned and unmanned lunar voyages beyond the Apollo program will be based on the results of these missions.

2. We should move ahead with bold exploration of the planets and the universe. In the next few years, scientific satellites of many types will be launched into Earth orbit to bring us new information about the universe, the solar system, and even our own planet. During the next decade, we will also launch unmanned spacecraft to all the planets of our solar system, including an unmanned vehicle which will be sent to land on Mars and to investigate its surface. In the late 1970's, the "Grand Tour" missions will study the mysterious outer planets of the solar system-Jupiter, Saturn, Uranus, Neptune, and Pluto. The positions of the planets at that time will give us a unique opportunity to launch missions which can visit several of them on a single flight of over 3 billion miles. Preparations for this program will begin in 1972.

There is one major but longer-range goal we should keep in mind as we proceed with our exploration of the planets. As a part of this program we will eventually send men to explore the planet Mars.

3. We should work to reduce substantially the cost of space operations. Our present rocket technology will provide a reliable launch capability for some time. But as we build for the longer-range future, we must devise less costly and less complicated ways of transporting payloads into space. Such a capability--designed so that it will be suitable for a wide range of scientific, defense, and commercial uses--can help us realize important economies in all aspects of our space program. We are currently examining in greater detail the feasibility of reusable space shuttles as one way of achieving this objective.

4. We should seek to extend man's capability to live and work in space. The Experimental Space Station (XSS)--a large orbiting workshop--will be an important part of this effort. We are now building such a station--using systems originally developed for the Apollo program--and plan to begin using it for operational missions in the next few years. We expect that men will be working in space for months at a time during the coming decade.

We have much to learn about what man can and cannot do in space. On the basis of our experience with the XSS, we will decide when and how to develop longer-lived space stations. Flexible, long-lived space station modules could provide a multipurpose space platform for the longer-range future and ultimately become a building block for manned interplanetary travel.

5. We should hasten and expand the practical applications of space technology. The development of Earth resources satellites--platforms which can help in such varied tasks as surveying crops, locating mineral deposits, and measuring water resources--will enable us to assess our environment and use our resources more effectively. We should continue to pursue other applications of space-related technology in a wide variety of fields, including meteorology, communications, navigation, air traffic control, education, and national defense. The very act of reaching into space can help man improve the quality of life on Earth.

6. We should encourage greater international cooperation in space. In my address to the United Nations last September, I indicated that the United States will take positive, concrete steps toward internationalizing man's epic venture into space--an adventure that belongs not to one nation but to all mankind. I believe that both the adventures and the applications of space missions should be shared by all peoples. Our progress will be faster, and our

accomplishments will be greater if nations will join together in this effort, both in contributing the resources and in enjoying the benefits. Unmanned scientific payloads from other nations already make use of our space launch capability on a cost-shared basis; we look forward to the day when these arrangements can be extended to larger applications, satellites and astronaut crews. The Administrator of NASA recently met with the space authorities of Western Europe, Canada, Japan, and Australia in an effort to find ways in which we can cooperate more effectively in space.[15]

The message seems to be an endorsement of much of the recommendations of the Space Task Force. However the writing was already on the wall insofar as large-scale space projects in the 1970s. By the time Nixon had issued this statement, the Apollo 20 mission had already been cancelled. Apollos 18 and 19 would follow it to the chopping block. The only vestige of the Apollo Applications Project that survived was Skylab, the space station that hosted three crews of three astronauts after Apollo 17's last flight to the Moon.

Nixon did wind up endorsing the space shuttle project.[16] Despite congressional reluctance to fund expensive space projects, the president concluded that the United States could not *not* have a space program. Ending human space

---

[15] Statement About the Future of the United States Space Program, President Richard Nixon, The American Presidency Project, 3/7/1970.
[16] The Space Shuttle Decision, T. E. Happenheimer, Chapter Nine: Nixon's Decision, National Space Society, 7/30/2008.

flight entirely would have devastated America's aerospace industry. The space shuttle would provide a practical benefit for the space program, lowering the cost of space travel which, in turn, would make future space missions, such as a space station, more feasible. Nevertheless the space shuttle was barely approved by Congress in 1972.

In any event, this meant that any post-Apollo lunar expeditions would be delayed indefinitely. While there have been a number of attempts to jump-start a return to the Moon program, these efforts, thus far, have floundered on the shoals of politics. The last human being to walk on the moon departed in December, 1972. No one has been back since.

As John Logsdon noted in his book, *After Apollo*,[17] President Nixon changed the concept of a space program as a national priority, first developed by President Kennedy, by downgrading it to just another government program. Space would still have some importance but would have to compete with other priorities for limited government dollars and attention. The course of the space program has been affected, some would say afflicted, by that shift ever since.

---

[17] After Apollo, John Logsdon, Palgrave Macmillan, 2015.

The Space Exploration Initiative

The optics could not have been better in front of the Air and Space Museum in Washington D. C. on July 20, 1989, which was the 20th anniversary of the Apollo 11 moon landing. President George H. W. Bush shared the stage with the three men who had made that voyage: Neil Armstrong, Buzz Aldrin, and Michael Collins. The president's remarks were, naturally, a lyrical recounting of the day men landed on the Moon. But then he proposed a new endeavor.

"In 1961 it took a crisis -- the space race -- to speed things up. Today we don't have a crisis; we have an opportunity. To seize this opportunity, I'm not proposing a 10-year plan like Apollo; I'm proposing a long-range, continuing commitment. First, for the coming decade, for the 1990's: Space Station Freedom, our critical next step in all our space endeavors. And next, for the new century: Back to the Moon; back to the future. And this time, back to stay. And then a journey into tomorrow, a journey to another planet: a manned mission to Mars."[18]

To Bush it seemed to be the perfect occasion to announce a new push for space exploration. The Cold War was winding down, though the extent of the collapse of the Soviet Union would not be apparent for several months. That meant that there would be both a peace dividend and a need for America's aerospace industry to have something to do besides build the weapons that might have been needed to fight the USSR.

---

[18] George H.W. Bush Announces the Space Exploration Initiative, July 20, 1989, YouTube.

Bush was also personally supportive of space exploration. Partly, this was because he called Texas home, having been a United States congressman from that state in the late 1960s. Partly, it was because space exploration appealed to both a sense of patriotism and a sense of adventure. It did not pass unnoticed that, just as Kennedy was identified with the first moon landing, Bush might be identified with the first Mars landing.

The Bush Space Exploration Initiative had its origins in the reports of two government commissions that took place during the administration of his predecessor, President Ronald Reagan. The National Commission on Space was appointed by Reagan in the wake of the *Challenger* explosion to map out a new direction for the United States space program. Its report, "Pioneering the Space Frontier,"[19] mapped out a coherent program that included a lunar base and human expeditions to Mars. NASA created its own task force, chaired by Dr. Sally Ride, the first American woman in space, to respond to the Pioneering the Space Frontier report. Its report, entitled "Leadership and America's Future in Space," also known as the Ride Report, mapped out four options for NASA's next great project:

> Mission to Planet Earth: a program designed to obtain a comprehensive scientific understanding of the entire Earth system— particularly emphasizing the impact of environmental changes on humanity.

> Exploration of the Solar System: a robotic exploration program designed to continue

[19] Pioneering the Space Frontier, the Report of the National Commission on Space, 1987

the quest to understand our planetary system (including a comet rendezvous, a mission to Saturn, and three sample return missions to Mars)

Outpost on the Moon: a program designed to build upon the Apollo legacy with a new phase of lunar exploration and development, concluding with the establishment of a permanent moon base by 2010.

Humans to Mars: a program designed to land a crew of astronauts early in the 21st century and eventually develop an outpost on the red planet.[20]

It was clear that the Bush administration was on solid policy grounds when it decided to develop and propose what became the Space Exploration Initiative. Pursuing a large-scale space exploration program would give America's aerospace sector something to do as the Cold War began to wind down. It would also have many of the same diplomatic, scientific, and economic benefits that were seen as having come from the Apollo program. But a number of policy and political mistakes conspired to throttle SEI in the crib. Congress never seriously funded the effort. When the Clinton administration came into office four years later, it quietly killed what was left of the second big effort to explore space beyond low Earth orbit.

Why did SEI, so enthusiastically begun, die such a miserable death? A number of theories abound, but Thor Hogan, in his study, "The Mars Wars,"[21] suggests that one

---

[20] Leadership and America's Future in Space, A Report to the NASA Administrator by Dr. Sally K. Ride August 1987.

of the crucial mistakes made by the Bush White House was to not vet the proposal with the various aerospace stakeholders, especially Congress, which would be expected to appropriate the extra money to pay for it. It was only inevitable that the Bush administration was blindsided by the vehement and angry opposition that the exploration initiative got in the Democrat-controlled Congress.

Furthermore NASA, in the now-infamous "90-Day Study,"[22] developed a plan that would take 30 years to implement and would cost $500 billion. This had the effect of poisoning the well for space exploration beyond low Earth orbit for decades. It empowered congressional appropriators such as Rep. Bob Traxler and Sen. Barbara Mikulski to, in effect, kill Bush's space exploration program before it had a chance to be born. Indeed, Traxler went through NASA's budget and excised existing programs, small scale as they were, that had anything to do with sending humans to the Moon or Mars.

The Bush administration tried to jump-start the SEI, even going so far as to convene its own blue ribbon panel chaired by Thomas Stafford, a former NASA astronaut. The report, "America at the Threshold,"[23] offered a number of options for carrying out Bush's initiative for slightly less money than the NASA "90-Day Study" suggested, but still numbering in the hundreds of billions of dollars.

---

[21] Mars Wars: The Rise and Fall of the Space Exploration Initiative, Thor Hogan. NASA History Series, 1003.
[22] Report on the 90-Day Study on the Human Exploration of the Moon and Mars, NASA History Archive, November, 1989.
[23] America at the Threshold: America's Space Exploration Initiative, Report of the Synthesis Group, May 1991.

Another report,[24] issued by the so-called Augustine Committee, the first to go by that name, covered the entire space program, but insofar as what it termed "Mission from Planet Earth," it recommended a go as you pay approach, so that the pace of space exploration would be measured by the availability of funding. It also reaffirmed the goals of a lunar base and expeditions to Mars.

In the spring of 1992, Richard Truly, deemed to be insufficiently enthused about the Space Exploration Initiative, was replaced by Dan Goldin, an executive at TRW. Goldin's mandate was to overhaul NASA and salvage the Space Exploration Initiative. Goldin was unable to do the second task, mainly because the author of SEI, President George H. W. Bush, lost his bid for reelection to Bill Clinton, a man with a profound disinterest in space exploration. Nevertheless Goldin would wind up being the longest serving NASA administrator, lasting throughout both of Clinton's terms and well into the first term of President George W. Bush, the son of the president who appointed him. Despite a mercurial management style, Goldin was able to reform the way unmanned space probes were developed, under the "faster, better, cheaper" doctrine, resulting in numerous robotic expeditions starting in the 1990s.

In the end, the Space Exploration Initiative represented a lost opportunity to jump-start human space exploration at the conclusion of the Cold War. The end of SEI was pregnant with wistful what-ifs. What if Bush has been more politically adroit and vetted SEI with congressional and other stakeholders in advance? What if Bush had pushed

---

[24] Report on the Advisory Committee On the Future of the U.S. Space Program, December 1990.

harder for his program, especially in the afterglow of his popularity in the wake of the Gulf War? What if Bush had won a second term, with a mandate to pursue space exploration, among other policies?

To be sure, some, but sadly not all, of the lessons of the brief life and bitter death of the Space Exploration Initiative were learned and taken to heart by Bush's son, the second President George Bush. For over a decade, however, human space exploration beyond low Earth orbit was all but dead at NASA, representing lost time and a dream deferred once again.

This policy did not mean that lunar exploration was entirely moribund at the space agency during the 1990s. The Lunar Prospector probe flew in 1998 as part of NASA's low-cost Discovery program and returned a considerable amount of science from Earth's nearest neighbor. In 1995, then-NASA Administrator, Dan Goldin, instituted a study of a Human Lunar Return[25] project that would have been run as a low-cost "skunk works" program. Nothing came of the proposal, which would have returned astronauts to the Moon in 2001. It was quietly shelved in 1996.

The Vision for Space Exploration

---

[25] Lunar Base Studies in the 1990s: 1996 Human Lunar Return (HLR), Marcus Lindroos, National Space Society.

One might be forgiven for having a sense of déjà vu if one happened to be at NASA headquarters on January 14, 2004. There was another president named George Bush about to make an announcement of a space exploration program. The circumstances were just a little different. For one thing, the announcement was being made in the shadow of another space tragedy.

About a year before, the space shuttle *Columbia* broke up in the skies over Texas, killing its crew. It was the second space shuttle disaster to afflict NASA, caused as it turned out by damage to the heat resistant tiles on the leading edge of the spacecraft's left wing. Besides the usual soul searching resulting from the accident investigation, the *Columbia* disaster caused a reevaluation of what the purpose of the civil space program was in the Bush administration.

Learning something from the mistakes of the previous Bush administration, the second Bush White House vetted the idea of a new space exploration plan with various stakeholders, including members of Congress who would be called upon to appropriate money for it. It also proposed a number of controversial cost-saving measures, including ending the space shuttle program by 2010 and the space station program by 2016 in order to help pay for the new program.

The younger Bush's speech announcing the program, which would soon be called the Vision for Space Exploration, was slightly lower key than that of his father. It took place at NASA headquarters before a selected audience.

Today I announce a new plan to explore space and extend a human presence across our solar system. We will begin the effort quickly, using existing programs and personnel. We'll make steady progress -- one mission, one voyage, one landing at a time.

Our first goal is to complete the International Space Station by 2010. We will finish what we have started, we will meet our obligations to our 15 international partners on this project. We will focus our future research aboard the station on the long-term effects of space travel on human biology. The environment of space is hostile to human beings. Radiation and weightlessness pose dangers to human health, and we have much to learn about their long-term effects before human crews can venture through the vast voids of space for months at a time. Research on board the station and here on Earth will help us better understand and overcome the obstacles that limit exploration. Through these efforts we will develop the skills and techniques necessary to sustain further space exploration.

To meet this goal, we will return the Space Shuttle to flight as soon as possible, consistent with safety concerns and the recommendations of the *Columbia* Accident Investigation Board. The Shuttle's chief purpose over the next several years will be to help finish assembly of the International Space Station. In 2010, the Space Shuttle -- after nearly 30 years of duty -- will be retired from service.

Our second goal is to develop and test a new spacecraft, the Crew Exploration Vehicle, by 2008, and to conduct the first manned mission no later than 2014. The Crew Exploration Vehicle will be capable of ferrying astronauts and scientists to the Space Station after the shuttle is retired. But the main purpose of this spacecraft will be to carry astronauts beyond our orbit to other worlds. This will be the first spacecraft of its kind since the Apollo Command Module.

Our third goal is to return to the moon by 2020, as the launching point for missions beyond. Beginning no later than 2008, we will send a series of robotic missions to the lunar surface to research and prepare for future human exploration. Using the Crew Exploration Vehicle, we will undertake extended human missions to the Moon as early as 2015, with the goal of living and working there for increasingly extended periods. Eugene Cernan, who is with us today -- the last man to set foot on the lunar surface -- said this as he left: 'We leave as we came, and God willing as we shall return, with peace and hope for all mankind.' America will make those words come true. (Applause.)

Returning to the Moon is an important step for our space program. Establishing an extended human presence on the Moon could vastly reduce the costs of further space exploration, making possible ever more ambitious missions. Lifting heavy spacecraft and fuel out of the Earth's gravity is expensive. Spacecraft assembled and provisioned on the Moon could escape its far lower gravity using far less energy, and thus, far less cost. Also, the Moon is home to abundant resources. Its soil contains raw materials that might be harvested and processed into rocket fuel or breathable air. We can use our time on the Moon to develop and test new approaches and technologies and systems that will allow us to function in other, more challenging environments. The Moon is a logical step toward further progress and achievement.

With the experience and knowledge gained on the Moon, we will then be ready to take the next steps of space exploration: human missions to Mars and to worlds beyond. (Applause.) Robotic missions will serve as trailblazers -- the advanced guard to the unknown. Probes, landers and other vehicles of this kind continue to prove their worth, sending spectacular images and vast amounts of data back to Earth. Yet the human thirst for knowledge ultimately cannot be satisfied by even the most vivid pictures, or the most detailed measurements.

We need to see and examine and touch for
ourselves. And only human beings are
capable of adapting to the inevitable
uncertainties posed by space travel.[26]

For the first year of its existence, what became the Vision
for Space Exploration made a good start. To be sure, there
were some detractors in Congress.[27] The House
Appropriators even trimmed NASA's budget by $1.1
billion dollars. This elicited the very first veto threat that
the Bush administration ever made. But it turned out not to
be necessary. The appropriations for NASA were folded
into an omnibus spending bill by late 2004. Then House
Majority Leader, Tom DeLay, whose district included
NASA's Johnson Spaceflight Center, threatened to scuttle
the entire spending bill unless NASA got every penny it
needed. The act of political hardball worked, and the space
exploration program got off to a good start.

As had become a tradition for new space exploration, a
presidential commission was created to map out a strategy
for the implementation of the Vision for Space Exploration.
It went by the long name of the President's Commission on
Implementation of United States Space Exploration Policy.
It was more commonly called the Aldridge Commission
after its chairman, Edward Aldridge, who had held a
number of government posts, including Secretary of the Air
Force, and jobs in the aerospace industry, including CEO of
the Aerospace Corporation. The commission included a
number of scientists such as Neil deGrasse Tyson and Paul

---

[26] President Bush Announced New Vision for Space Exploration
Program, White House, 1/14/2004.
[27] Delay's Push Helps Deliver NASA Funds, Guy Gugliotta, The
Washington Post, 12/6/2004.

Spudis, former politicians like Robert Walker, and business CEOs like Carly Florina.

The report of the Aldridge Commission [28]was issued fairly quickly, on June 4, 2004. The report contained a number of recommendations to organize NASA and private industry around President Bush's space exploration vision, as well as to provide incentives for commercial space development. The report also recommended the development of a heavy-lift launcher as well as technology to extract and use extraterrestrial resources to facilitate the exploration vision. Above all the effort needed to be "sustainable," which at the time meant that it would survive several presidential administrations and congresses.

Paul Spudis, a lunar scientist who served on the Aldridge Commission, would later write about what came next and why; ultimately, the Vision for Space Exploration lost direction and was eventually killed by the Obama administration.[29]

The first disturbing development occurred as NASA conducted its own study on how to fulfill the requirements of the VSE. In Spudis' view, NASA was taking a perfunctory view toward the Moon and was regarding it as a place to stop briefly before heading for the true destination, Mars.

Yet another study,[30] conducted for the Planetary Society, was aimed at Mars, though it also mentioned the Moon and

---

[28] A Journey to Inspire, Innovate, and Discover, Report of the President's Commission on Implementation of United States Space Policy, June 2004.
[29]The Vision for Space Exploration: A Brief History (Part 2), Spudis Lunar Resources Blog, Dr. Paul Spudis, 10/26/2012
[30] Extending Human Presence Into the Solar System. The Planetary

other destinations as crucial places to go. It concluded that a new heavy-lift launcher was crucial for realizing dreams of exploration beyond low Earth orbit. This is significant because Michael Griffin, who had been associate administrator for exploration during the Space Exploration Initiative era, was one of the Planetary Society study team co-leaders. Griffin replaced Sean O'Keefe as administrator of NASA in April, 2005. He immediately set about forging the direction for the VSE specifically and the space agency in general.

Griffin set about incorporating some of the work he did for the Planetary Society Study into the implementation plan for the Vision for Space Exploration. He ordered an internal study called the Exploration Systems Architecture Study[31] which was released in November, 2005. It put into effect a number of changes in the plan to implement VSE that had been developed under the O'Keefe era. First, instead of a fly-off between two versions of a Crewed Exploration Vehicle, essentially a 21st century version of an Apollo capsule, there would be only one version developed from the start. Also, technology development for new rocket boosters that would be needed for the exploration program would be kept to a minimum. Shuttle derived and other existing technology would be used as much as possible. The idea was to reduce the time and cost of developing the architecture to be used for the space exploration program.

What emerged from this study were the following space craft and rockets:

Society, July, 2004.
[31] NASA's Exploration Systems Architecture Study, November 2005.

- The Orion, which was a four-person space capsule in which the astronauts would ride into low Earth orbit.
- The Ares 1, a rocket booster that would launch the Orion.
- The Ares V, a super-heavy-lift rocket that would carry the rest of the spacecraft and would be needed for a lunar surface expedition.
- The Altair lunar lander, which would take the four-person crew to and from the Moon.
- The Earth Departure Stage that would send the Orion and Altair from low Earth orbit to lunar orbit.

With the space shuttle program scheduled to end in 2010, the plan was to get the Orion and Ares 1 up and running by 2012 in order to take crews to and from the International Space Station. In parallel, NASA conducted a Commercial Orbital Transportation System program that would develop the first commercially-run cargo spacecraft and then a crewed spacecraft. The idea was that commercial companies in the program would be partners with NASA, developing their own spacecraft with the space agency contributing some funding. If any of the commercial vehicles came to fruition, one or more of them would take over the task of servicing the ISS.

The first lunar mission was envisioned to take place in 2019, in time for the 50th anniversary of the Apollo 11 lunar landing. The Ares 1 would lift four astronauts into low Earth orbit on board an Orion. Around the same time, the Ares V would lift the Altair lunar lander and the EDS into low Earth orbit. The Altair/EDS would dock with the Orion in Earth orbit. After a checkout period, the EDS would fire its engines and blast the Orion/Altair to the

Moon. Three days later, the spacecraft would assume lunar orbit. The four astronauts would transfer to the Altair, leaving the Orion in automatic mode. They would descend to the lunar surface and make a landing. Soon after, the first human beings would walk on the Moon since 1972. The astronauts would stay a week before returning.

The report also mentioned the idea of an asteroid mission, likely substituting a habitation module for the lunar lander. The eventual mission to Mars was not well defined but would likely have included concepts of the "Mars Direct" plan, which was first developed by Dr. Robert Zubrin.

Two things happened between the release of the ESAS report and the end of the Bush administration. First, technical challenges involving the construction of hardware needed to begin deep space operations began to crop up, delaying a number of milestones. Second, NASA ran into the desire, by Bush's Office of Management and Budget, to cut NASA's funding below the amount that Griffin and the Bush administration agreed would be needed to execute Constellation on time.

According to a story in the Washington Post,[32] NASA and OMB were at loggerheads over the amount of funding the space agency would get and even what Griffin could say in congressional testimony about things like China's lunar ambitions. Evidently, some parts of the Bush administration that wanted to rein in NASA spending were fearful that Griffin, who enjoyed a great deal of credibility in Congress, would persuade that body to allocate more money above the White House request if he sounded the

---

[32] NASA's Star is Fading, Its Chief Says, Marc Kaufman, Washington Post, 9/14/2008.

alarm about a possible return to the Moon by China before the United States.

The End of Constellation

The Bush administration ended in January 2009. The new president, Barack Obama, had a political philosophy and a view toward space exploration that was decidedly different from that of his predecessor. During the campaign he had supported delaying Constellation for five years to fund an educational initiative. He later backtracked on the pledge when it was pointed out that it would involve extending the "space flight gap" between the end of the space shuttle program and whatever came next, a commercial space taxi or an Orion, to take astronauts into space,[33] In a space policy paper released by his campaign, Obama endorsed returning to the Moon by 2020 in advance of going to Mars.[34]

Obama did not move against the Constellation program right away. First he convened a presidential commission, headed by retired aerospace executive, Norm Augustine. The final report[35] was issued in October of 2009, and concluded that the Constellation project was so underfunded and behind schedule that it had become unexecutable. It offered two main options for space exploration going forward. Moon First would preserve the overall goals of Constellation but would cancel the two Ares rockets, which would be replaced by a single heavy-lift rocket. Flexible Path would bypass the Moon for the time being and focus on Earth-approaching asteroids, the

---

[33] Obama Pits Human Space Exploration against Education, Loretta Hidalgo Whitesides, Wired, 11/21/2007.

[34]Advancing the Frontiers of Space Exploration, Obama08 Campaign Document

[35] Seeking a Human Spaceflight Program Worthy of a Great Nation, Review of U.S. Spaceflight Plans Committee, October, 2009.

moons of Mars, the Lagrange Points between the Earth and the Moon and the Earth and the Sun. Both options were designed to lead to an eventual mission to Mars.

The second Augustine Committee recommended that NASA's budget should be increased by $3 billion a year, Among the other recommendations were: extending the International Space Station to 2020 and going all in for a government-financed, commercially-operated transportation system to take cargo and astronauts to and from the ISS.

The other shoe fell on February 1, 2010, with the release of the FY 2011 budget proposal. The Obama administration proposed killing the Constellation program entirely and, instead, funding a six billion-dollar project for a commercially-developed spacecraft that would replace the space shuttle and take astronauts to and from the International Space Station.[36] NASA would conduct a development program for "game-changing" exploration technology, including a new, as yet undefined, heavy-lift launcher.

The congressional reaction was swift, bipartisan, and mainly negative. The entire Florida congressional delegation sent a letter to President Obama decrying the decision to terminate Constellation.[37] The letter noted that the Constellation program enjoyed wide, bipartisan support in Congress. It expressed a number of concerns, including whether a commercial spacecraft could be viable without a

---

[36] Obama 2011 budget request: Major Shakeup for NASA, Joel Achenbach, Washington Post, 2/1/2010.
[37] Florida Congressional Delegation Letter to President Obama Regarding NASA FY 2011 Budget, SpaceRef, 3/4/2010.

publicly-operated backup as planned under the Constellation program.

Certainly, the members of Congress who attacked the cancellation of Constellation, especially those from space states such as Florida, Texas, and Alabama, could be accused of protecting jobs in the district. However, the Obama administration made a crucial mistake, the same one that President George H. W. Bush made when he proposed the Space Exploration Initiative. It did not consult Congress or any of the other aerospace stakeholders when it made the decision to kill Constellation. It simply gave the order and expected everyone to fall into line without complaint, underestimating the level of support the program enjoyed.

The termination of Constellation did get some support from commercial space advocates, such as SpaceX's Elon Musk, whose company stood to benefit immensely from the new plan. And even many supporters of space exploration beyond low Earth orbit had their reservations about Constellation. It had been underfunded and would have taken a great deal of money to get back on track.

However, the Augustine Committee did provide a way to end Constellation and still preserve its essential goals in the Moon First Option. The sticking point was that the Obama administration was unwilling to spend the extra $3 billion a year that going to the Moon or pursuing the so-called Flexible Path option would cost. This was remarkable, considering that, the previous year, the administration passed a nearly $900 billion stimulus package that was intended to get the moribund economy started again.

President Obama's decision to cancel Constellation contrasts rather unfavorably with how President Bill Clinton dealt with the Space Station Freedom project. When Clinton came into office, in 1993, his administration decided that Freedom had become unexecutable, much as the Obama administration did regarding Constellation. However, instead of cancelling the project outright, the Clinton administration restructured it into the program that became the International Space Station and brought in the Russian Federation in a full partnership. The ISS was duly built and is hosting crews and returning good science and technology development to this day.

It is clear that had Obama followed the Clinton approach by replacing Constellation with something along the lines of Moon First, as suggested by Augustine, he would have avoided a great deal of the political acrimony and turmoil that continues to plague the space agency. Why he did not follow the example of his predecessor remains open to conjecture, but one can reach the inescapable conclusion that he is not very supportive of the idea of space exploration.

The negative reaction against the President's space policy was so heated that Obama was obliged to travel to the Kennedy Space Center and give a speech to a selected audience, which included Apollo astronaut Buzz Aldrin who supported the policy. In the speech, Obama added the goal of visiting an Earth-approaching asteroid as a preliminary destination on the way to a human expedition to Mars.

The president had no patience with those critics who wanted America to return to the Moon. He stated, "Now, I understand that some believe that we should attempt a return to the surface of the Moon first, as previously planned. But I just have to say pretty bluntly here: We've been there before. Buzz has been there. There's a lot more of space to explore, and a lot more to learn when we do."[38]

The speech did very little to mollify the critics of the President's space policy. Three of the most celebrated, then-living Apollo astronauts, Neil Armstrong, the first man to walk on the Moon, Gene Cernan, the last man to walk on the Moon, and Jim Lovell, the commander of the Apollo 13 mission, had already penned a letter before the President's speech decrying the decision to abandon the Moon.[39] Armstrong and Cernan reiterated their critique in testimony to the Senate Commerce Committee less than a month later.[40]

Congress was singularly unimpressed by the President's speech or by after-the-fact defenses of Constellation's cancellation. Instead of studying the development of a heavy-lift launcher, Congress mandated the development of the Space Launch System, comprising technology from both the space shuttle and the Saturn V. Along with it, Congress insisted on the building of the Orion Multi-Purpose Crew Vehicle that would be launched on the SLS

[38] Remarks by the President on Space Exploration in the 21st Century, President Barack Obama, 4/15/2010.
[39] Armstrong: Obama NASA Plan 'devastating', NBC Nightly News with Brian Williams, 4/13/2010.
[40] Astronauts Neil Armstrong, Eugene Cernan oppose Obama's spaceflight plans, Ed O'Keefe and Marc Kaufman, Washington Post, May 12, 2010.
[41] National Aeronautics and Space Administration Authorization Act of 2010.

to destinations beyond low Earth orbit. These mandates were incorporated into the 2010 NASA Authorization Act.[41]

The act represented a messy compromise between President Obama and Congress. It did not preserve the Constellation program, but it did list the lunar surface as one of the destinations where Americans should go. It incorporated several features of the President's space policy, such as a commercial crew program to replace the space shuttle and extending the International Space Station to at least 2020.

The Fallout of the Obama Space Policy

The passage of the 2010 NASA authorization bill did not extinguish the controversy surrounding the cancellation of Project Constellation. Some commercial space advocates, such as Rick Tumlinson, the founder of the Space Frontier Foundation and Deep Space Industries, an asteroid mining company, slammed the heavy-lift rocket as the "Senate Launch System."[42] The critics of the SLS contended that it is an expensive boondoggle imposed on the space agency by Congress to preserve jobs in the district. Opponents of the SLS included the then-Deputy Administrator of NASA, Lori Garver, who discreetly declined to make her opposition known until after she left the space agency.[43]

Opponents of the Space Launch System pointed to an internal NASA study[44] that suggested that space exploration voyages could be undertaken by existing or soon-to-exist rockets. The idea was that several launches would be executed to supply an orbiting fuel depot. Then a spacecraft would be launched, would top off at the fuel depot, and then proceed to its destination, the lunar surface or an Earth-approaching asteroid. The expense of creating a heavy-lift rocket would be avoided. Proponents also claimed that the fuel depot plan would be cheaper because high flight rates for the commercial rockets such as the SpaceX Falcon Heavy and the United Launch Alliance Delta IV Heavy would make launch costs decline further.

---

[42] The Senate Launch System, Rick Tumlinson, the Huffington Post, 4/2/2011.
[43] Huntsville-designed Space Launch System should be killed, former NASA No. 2 Lori Garver says, Lee Roop, AL.com, 1.3.2014.
[44] Propellants Depot Requirements Study Report, HAT Technical Interchange Meeting, 7/21/2011.

The fuel depot scheme had one glaring flaw. Since it would take nine launches of a Falcon Heavy to support a single asteroid mission and six to support a lunar surface mission, only three or four deep space missions could be supported in a single decade. The commercial rockets cited in the study could not achieve the flight rate necessary to manage anything more robust.

President Obama's bold mission to an asteroid morphed, as time went on, into the Asteroid Redirect Mission.[45] Instead of sending a crew of astronauts to an Earth-approaching asteroid, the plan became using a robotic spacecraft to capture either a small asteroid or a boulder from a larger asteroid and place it in lunar orbit. Then an Orion spacecraft would be launched on a Space Launch System to rendezvous with the small asteroid and explore it, taking samples, and then returning to Earth.

The reaction to the Asteroid Redirect Mission (ARM) was, to say the least, very negative from observers outside NASA. The National Research Council recommended in a report, "Pathways to Exploration,"[46] that the ARM be scrapped and replaced by either a return to the Moon or an expedition to an asteroid "in its native orbit." Richard Binzel, a professor at MIT and a world authority on asteroids, slammed the idea, stating that it had no scientific merit and would not contribute anything to an expedition to Mars.[47] Its only justifications were that it would take American astronauts beyond low Earth orbit and that it would be cheap.

---

[45] Asteroid Redirect Mission Overview, Robert M. Lightfoot, NASA Associated Administrator.
[46] Pathways to Exploration, National Research Council, 2014.
[47] Is NASA's "Asteroid Redirect Mission" Worthless? Joshua Filmer, Quarks and Quasars, 8/6/2014.

The Moon was not entirely forgotten, either by NASA or politicians in Washington. NASA floated a proposal called the Deep Space Station[48] that would involve deploying a space station at the Earth/Moon Lagrange 2 point. The Deep Space Station would be situated over the lunar far side and would be human tended. It would serve as a way station for voyages from Earth to virtually any destination in the solar system, including the lunar surface.

Astronauts would be able to visit the Deep Space Station periodically and then ride a reusable landing craft to the lunar surface. Once a fuel manufacturing operation began at a moon base, using ice water mined from the lunar poles, the Deep Space Station would become a refueling base, with rocket fuel conveyed from the lunar surface to top off spacecraft headed to other destinations in the solar system such as Mars or back to Earth.

Unfortunately, as elegant a solution to the problem of an interplanetary transportation infrastructure as the Deep Space Station would represent, the Obama administration was singularly unimpressed. Building the Deep Space Station would have cost more money than the administration was willing to spend, based on previous administration policy.

The Moon came up during the Republican primary contest in early 2012 when presidential candidate and former House Speaker Newt Gingrich proposed the establishment of a moon base by 2020.[49] He offered few details except

---

[48] NASA Eyes Plan for Deep-Space Outpost Near the Moon, Leonard David, Space.com, 2/10/2012.
[49] Newt Pledges Moon Base by Second Term, Alexander Burns, Politico, 1/25.2012.

that the base would be entirely American and would be largely commercial.

While Gingrich's moon base proposal garnered a positive response in aerospace circles, it was not the case on the campaign trail. Mitt Romney, the former governor of Massachusetts, mercilessly mocked the proposal, stating during a debate, "If I had a business executive come to me and say I want to spend a few hundred billion dollars to put a colony on the Moon, I'd say, 'You're fired.'"[50]

Romney's jibe was odd for a number of reasons. For one thing, a moon base was public policy between 2004 and 2010 as part of the Constellation program. For another thing, Romney had been endorsed by a number of aerospace heavy hitters, many of whom were return to the Moon advocates, such as former NASA administrator, Mike Griffin, and Apollo 17 astronaut, Gene Cernan.[51]

Nevertheless the ridicule worked. The normally erudite Gingrich seemed unable to come up with a coherent response to Romney's ridicule. The moon base proposal was even the subject of a skit on *Saturday Night Live*.[52] The proposal and, shortly thereafter, the Gingrich candidacy sank out of sight.

Ironically, three and a half years later, a NASA-funded study[53] concluded that a commercially-run lunar base was

---

[50] Romney Mocks Gingrich's Plan for Moon Base, CBS News Tampa Bay/AP, 1/26/2012.
[51] Space Execs Hope to Rocket Romney, Kevin Liptak, CNN, 1/27/2012.
[52] SNL Gingrich Moon Colony Cold Open (Video), Huffington Post, 2/6/2012.
[53] NexGen Space LLC Page 1 Evolvable Lunar Architecture Economic Assessment and Systems Analysis of an Evolvable Lunar Architecture

doable for, not hundreds of billions of dollars, but for $10 billion. Moreover, the first moon boots could be on the lunar soil as early as 2021. The fact that Gingrich did not have such a detailed analysis, vetted by some of the best space experts in America, to buttress his proposal must be the bitterest of ironies.

Efforts to refocus American space exploration back to the Moon nevertheless continued in Congress. A number of Congress members introduced a bill, entitled "The Reasserting American Leadership in Space Act" or the REAL Space Act.[54] The bill would mandate that NASA redirect its space exploration efforts toward a return to the Moon in order to establish a "permanent presence." As of this writing it has not gotten out of committee.

---

that Leverages Commercial Space Capabilities and Public-Private-Partnerships, NextGen Space LLC, July 13, 2015.
[54] HR 1446: The Real Space Act, Thomas.gov

Why is Returning to the Moon so Hard?

The question as to why no one has been back to the Moon since December, 1972, is a vexing one. Certainly the United States has both the technical wherewithal and the economic strength to send astronauts back. Two American presidents, both coincidentally named George Bush, attempted to start long-term space exploration efforts that would have included a return to the Moon. Both efforts were ended prematurely.

Why was it that President Kennedy succeeded in getting a lunar program started, and subsequent presidents failed to replicate that feat? The conventional wisdom is that the early 1960s were ripe for a space race to the Moon, with the Cold War going full bore and fears that the Soviet Union would demonstrate its superiority in the heavens. That incentive did not exist either in 1989 or 2004. Like most conventional wisdom, this analysis is true, up to a point.

The reasons for the failures of the Space Exploration Initiative that was announced by President George H. W. Bush, in 1989, and the Vision for Space Exploration that was announced by President George W. Bush, in 2004, included political and leadership failures which, had they been avoided, might well have saved those programs from cancelation. True, both space exploration programs were cancelled by Democratic presidents who succeeded the presidents named Bush. But Clinton, in the first instance, and Obama, in the second, were able to get away with this because of structural problems that the two programs had run into.

Many historians have concluded that the Apollo program survived as long as it did because it had become a memorial to the slain President John F. Kennedy. Kennedy's death certainly stopped attempts to throttle Apollo in its crib. The question of whether Kennedy could have fended off attempts to cut the program had he lived is best left to alternate history creators. The answer depends on how much political capital he would have been willing to spend to fend off the budget cutters to keep the program going. The one thing that is clear is that starting and maintaining a large-scale space program is dependent on two things.

First, it is helpful if the political zeitgeist lends itself to such a space program. The Cold War served to sustain the Apollo program. The need to keep NASA as a functioning agency saved the space shuttle in the 1970s. The space station almost failed until President Bill Clinton used it to help transition Russia from its Soviet superpower status peacefully and to give Russian engineers something to do besides work for rogue regimes such as Iran and North Korea. It can also be argued that President George H. W. Bush proposed the Space Exploration Initiative too soon. The space station project was still controversial, in 1989, when Bush made his big speech. However, the International Space Station was a going concern in 2004 when the younger Bush rolled out the Vision for Space Exploration. With the death of the *Columbia* space shuttle and her crew, a feeling had arisen that astronauts should risk their lives for grander things than going in circles around the Earth.

Second, presidential leadership, strong, consistent, and long lasting, has to be present. Bush the elder made the mistake of not vetting the Space Exploration Initiative before announcing it just months into his administration. He was blindsided by the hostile reception it got in Congress, in the media, and even inside NASA. Had the elder Bush won a second term, he might have gotten his initiative off the ground. But that is another what-if scenario.

Bush the younger avoided some of the mistakes that his father and namesake made. His administration spent nearly a year between the *Columbia* accident and his big speech developing what became the Vision for Space Exploration, and he vetted it with Congress and various other aerospace stakeholders. Furthermore, Bush paid attention to his initiative for the first year after it was announced, even going so far as to issue his first veto threat to ensure that it was properly funded during its first year.

Unfortunately, President Bush's attention wandered. This is understandable as his administration was dealing with a grinding stalemate in Iraq and an impending economic calamity that burst onto the scene in the fall of 2008, just in time for the election of Bush's successor. The funding that was promised for the VSE was cut back, the program suffered some technical challenges, the milestones became delayed, and the criticism rose to a crescendo.

The VSE was also harmed by the election of Barack Obama to the presidency. Obama, protestations aside, is a man who is implacably hostile to the idea of space exploration. Despite the options offered by the Augustine Committee to fix some of the problems surrounding Project Constellation, Obama chose to terminate funding for it. It took heroic efforts in the Congress to preserve some parts of it and to compel the President to propose the asteroid mission some months later.

If VSE and Project Constellation had been better funded and had been seen as making more progress, it is possible that President Obama would not have dared to cancel it or, having attempted to do so, would have been stopped by the program's supporters in Congress. As it is, two crucial pieces of hardware, the Orion spacecraft and the heavy-lift Space Launch System, are in development for a return to the moon.

The question now arises, given those facts, how does an American president set in motion a return to the Moon program and successfully take it to a conclusion?

How to Return to the Moon

February, 2017…

The traditional way to announce a big space initiative is to make a big speech, sometimes before a joint session of Congress. John F. Kennedy famously launched mankind to the Moon in a special joint session. Ronald Reagan included the announcement for what eventually became the International Space Station during the State of the Union Address in 1984.

The next space initiative could happen like the following scenario.

Rumors abound even before the new president's inauguration that he intends to include a shift in space policy in his State of the Union proposals. Thus far, the White House has been close-mouthed about what that might be, but based on some statements made during the campaign, the scuttlebutt is that it will be a lunar effort.

The night's proceedings go ahead as many previous ones have. The Sergeant at Arms enters the packed House chamber and announces, "Mr. Speaker, the President of the United States!" As everyone in the room rises to their feet to applaud, the President, accompanied by a congressional escort, enters, making slow progress as he greets senators and congressmen.

Finally, the President arrives at the speaker's platform, greets the Vice-President and the Speaker of the House, and then assumes his place. The cheering gradually dies down, and everyone takes their seats.

The State of the Union Address is both the end of a long process and the beginning of a new one. The moment the new president is elected, he and his transition team interact with the Congressional leadership, vetting policy proposals, taking input and refining the same proposals based on that input. One of those proposals is the return to the Moon project. The media have already reported on the proposal, debated it, and critiqued it. Now the official rollout will occur.

The new president states his intention to send astronauts back to the Moon sometime after his tax and defense initiatives and before announcing the latest plan to reform the current health care reform regime.

"Next, I propose to redirect the space exploration efforts of NASA with a goal of returning American astronauts to the Moon no later than the year 2022, 50 years after the last Apollo mission. This effort will include the space agencies of other, friendly countries, as well as private business and academia. The goal will not just be exploration, but the economic development of what many have called the eighth continent. Let there be no illusions about this effort. There will be an added cost to it which will require the first significant increases in NASA's budget in decades. But I believe that, even as we struggle to restrain federal spending and jump-start a sluggish economy, the riches to be gained will be worth it.

"The lunar effort will involve the permanent presence of human beings on another world for the first time. I propose that a lunar outpost be created that will serve as a center of science and commerce that will benefit this country and all humankind.

"The lunar effort will enhance American leadership around the world. In this century, the countries that matter the most will be those who lead in the exploration and economic development of space. If America fails to lead, other countries, who lack our values of freedom and tolerance, will take up that leadership to the detriment of our planet.

"The Moon can be the source of economic wealth that will not only further exploration into deep space but will directly benefit the people of Earth. Water, in the form of ice, can be refined into rocket fuel for spacecraft to top off before proceeding to distant destinations like Mars. Platinum group and rare earth materials will help to feed our high-tech industries on both Earth and in new industrial facilities in space. The promise of helium-3, a substance not found in nature on Earth, could help fuel future fusion reactors, creating boundless sources of energy.

"The lunar effort will advance scientific discoveries beyond the realm of imagination. Exploring the Moon will further our understanding of the origin of our solar system. The lunar surface will also serve as the site of observatories that will make new discoveries far and beyond any that have been built before, on Earth and in space.

"The lunar base will also serve as a test bed for our eventual human exploration of Mars. We shall test the technology that we shall use to get to Mars and operate on its surface on the Moon and in cislunar space, days away from Earth rather than months.

"Finally, the lunar effort will fire the imagination and enthusiasm of young people, inspiring a new generation of scientists, engineers, and business entrepreneurs. It has been thus for previous frontiers and will be thus for the high frontier of space."

At that point, the chamber erupts in cheers, some more enthusiastic than others. The proposal has been made as it has so many times before. But the big speech will be just the beginning of a long, hard slog that will last, at least, until there are moon boots back on the lunar surface a little more than five years hence.

The slog, in fact, will have started on the cable news talk shows as panels of experts and pundits debated the merits of the President's various proposals and their likelihood of being accepted. Fox News will have been generally supportive, MSNBC less so. But everyone will have wondered if the new president could manage to get Congress to pass the funding necessary for a return to the moon, estimated to require a $23 billion NASA budget by 2020. However, the third attempt to return to the Moon since the last Apollo mission will have gotten off to a good start. The President will have laid out the reasons for making the proposal in stark, easy-to-understood terms. But now he will have to shepherd the project through Congress, a task easier said than done.

Selling the Plan – Dealing with Objections

Every president can make a good speech. It can be said that few people have ever achieved the presidency of the United States without the ability of speaking well. The secret to making a proposal, like a return to the Moon, a reality is not presenting it in a great speech. The secret is in selling it and making sure that it remains on track after the applause is over.

If the president is smart, he has already vetted his return to the Moon plan with the various interest groups who will have some say over it. These include members of Congress, the scientific community, the aerospace industry, and potential international partners. Having run the plan by the interest groups, the president will have a feel for how it will be received. Ideally he will have already lined up enough support to get the plan off the ground during the first year.

Opposition will still exist. People will raise objections. It behooves the president to anticipate such objections and to have well-researched answers for them. Newt Gingrich failed to take this step, in 2012, when he rolled out his lunar base plan and was subsequently blindsided when Mitt Romney ridiculed it, calling it a "zany" idea.

What kind of objections will be raised against a return to the moon? Here follows a brief and not necessarily complete list.

1. A return to the moon would cost too much in an era of large deficits. Every agency of the government, including NASA, must contribute to balancing the budget.

The answer to this objection will depend on what the state of the deficit is in 2017. If the deficit is on a downward course, presumably because of increased economic growth and spending restraint in other government accounts, the objection has less resonance. The president can point out the contributions NASA has given to the economy, partly through the development of technology that has been later adapted to other uses. He/She can also mention that any increase that the space agency needs to pay for a return to the Moon represents a rounding error in the amount of the deficit. The cause of the deficit is out of control spending on entitlements that have to be restrained.

2. How can you even think of spending money on space exploration when you're cutting back on spending for healthcare, education, and the environment?

The hidden presumption of this objection is that if we go back to the Moon or do any other large-scale space project that costs money, like a Mars expedition, people will die of diseases, children will not be educated, and the world will perish from global warming. This particular objection is tough to counter because it is designed not so much to raise a logical point as it is to elicit an emotional response. The proponent of a return to the Moon can use as many statistics and present as many facts as he wants to support the undertaking, but the images of starving children and dead senior citizens remain powerful. One way to defend against this line of attack is to go on the attack oneself, by pointing out how the very programs that have been used to address social problems have made them worse. One should also point out how a return to the Moon could help address these very same problems, from economic growth to education.

3. Why are we going back to the moon? We've already been there and have done that. We should be going to Mars instead.

The argument over what the next destination should be for space explorers has been going on for decades. The case for each place (the Moon, Mars, or an asteroid) have been articulated with great passion, with good arguments for each one. Two approaches exist for dealing with this argument. The first approach is to make the position that the Moon, by being nearby, is the best initial goal for astronaut explorers. Asteroids and/or Mars can come later, especially when more experience and technology have been developed. The second approach is to fund the Moon and Mars as parallel rather than sequential programs. In that way the argument is settled because both sides are satisfied. On the other hand, the near-term cost will be that much greater and thus more difficult to defend.

4. Robots can do the same sort of exploration for far less money and in better safety.

This sentiment has been around since the Apollo moon landing. It is not as widely believed in the scientific community as it once was. Refer to the Royal Astronomical Society study[55] when refuting this objection.

5. Going back to the Moon is the right goal, but NASA is doing it all wrong. Its approach is too expensive and unsustainable. There are better ways to do this that are only being rejected because it garners insufficient pork for certain members of Congress.

---

[55] Report on the Commission on the Scientific Case for Human Space Exploration, Royal Astronomical Society, 2004

One of the at once salutary and pernicious effects of the Internet is that it provides a forum for debate on any issue imaginable. During the Project Constellation era, a great many armchair rocket scientists maintained that the project, while worthy, was doomed to failure because of the choices of hardware that NASA had made. In general these objections can be safely ignored, unless someone important, a member of Congress, for example, starts to share them. In that case it is best to leave defending the technical details of the return to the Moon program to the NASA administrator and the engineers and managers whom he or she designates.

6. Going back to the moon is fine, but we really need to get away from the whole final frontier and American exceptionalism mythos. That kind of rhetoric smacks of conquest and exploitation, which implies colonialization. The rest of the world finds it offensive. We need to think of places like the Moon in the same way we think of Antarctica, as places to explore and study, but not places to economically develop or live on.

This thesis has been conspicuously advanced by a self-described aerospace communications expert named Dr. Linda Billings, most recently in a paper in *Scientific American* entitled "The Inexcusable Jingoism of American Spaceflight Rhetoric."[56] The idea is that the American frontier metaphor that many people use to describe what they wish to happen in space is outdated, politically incorrect, and out of step with the world community. The thesis is clearly ideologically motivated and should be treated as such. The return to the Moon effort will be

---

[56] The Inexcusable Jingoism of American Spaceflight Rhetoric, Dr. Linda Billings, Scientific America, 7/14/2015.

American led and therefore should conform to American values, which will need defending in this context. Freedom and free market capitalism are good things, whether practiced on Earth or in the high frontier of space.

Selling the Plan – Dealing with Congress

It is axiomatic that, without the support of Congress, a return to the Moon is not going to happen. Congress scuttled President George H. W. Bush's Space Exploration Initiative, in the early 1990s, by refusing to fund it. On the other hand, Congress supported President George W. Bush's Vision for Space Exploration after some initial prodding. Congress was instrumental in saving key parts of the VSE program after President Obama's attempt to kill it.

If the incoming president is smart, he/she will have already vetted a return to the Moon program with the congressional leadership. However, the first year is crucial for getting such a program off the ground. It is therefore useful to go over what needs to be done to make that happen.

Two sets of committees in Congress deal with NASA and how much money it gets. One set, called the authorization committees, consists of the House Science, Space, and Technology Committee and the Senate Commerce Committee. Also, both the House and Senate Appropriations Committees are central to deciding how much money the space agency receives each fiscal year.

The authorization committees each have a subcommittee that oversees NASA. In the House, this is the Space Subcommittee. In the Senate, this is the Science and Space Subcommittee. These subcommittees set NASA policy, crafting legislative language that defines the missions and direction that the space agency is charged with. They also set a funding authorization level, which is not the actual funding bill, but rather a kind of funding limit for the appropriators to work with.

The first thing that a president proposing to send American astronauts back to the Moon must do is to get the Congressional stamp of approval on the project by having the plan incorporated into the NASA Authorization Bill. This task should be relatively easy; while there will be a recommendation of how much money should be spent, the amount will not necessarily be binding on the appropriators.

The House and Senate appropriations committees will have a vital role in determining whether a return to the Moon takes off or is destroyed on launch. The appropriators determine how much money is spent by which department, agency, and bureau in the government. They also determine the level of funding for various accounts within those parts of the government. The appropriators can fully fund the return to the Moon program, partly fund it, or provide no money for the project.

One of the problems NASA has always had in getting adequate funding is that it competes for money with several other agencies and departments. This is because each subcommittee is allocated a certain amount of money that it can dispense among the various parts of the government under its purview. In both the Senate and the House, NASA competes with the Commerce and Justice Departments and certain other agencies, such as the National Science Foundation.

The appropriations process is supposed to follow a set pattern. The appropriations subcommittees in each house of Congress pass their version of a bill. Then, the full committees pass the bill, followed by the full House and Senate. Since the bills passed by the House and Senate are usually different, the differences are ironed out in a conference committee which then presents a unified bill that is passed by the two houses and then sent to the president for his signature.

More often than not, at least in recent years, Congress managed to complete only a few if any appropriations bills by the end of the fiscal year at the end of September. Then Congress scrambles to lump all of the unpassed spending bills into a catchall continuing resolution or even a series of continuing resolutions as various factions of the legislative branch and the White House negotiate about how much the government will spend. Sometimes the work is not done until the end of the actual year, whereupon the process starts all over again.

The sad fact of the matter is that the budget process is designed to allow for maximum mischief making at every step of the way. Usually this involves adding in more spending. But sometimes the mischief consists of attacking the president's priorities, greatly reducing what is spent on them, or canceling them outright.

Influencing members of Congress to support a presidential priority is an art. The process of bending a politician to the presidential will is dependent as much on the president as it is the politician being influenced. According to *Dead Presidents*,[57] President Lyndon Johnson would use something called "the treatment" to bend people to his will. He would use his large, physical size and his intimidating personality to convince a senator or congressman to vote the way he wanted. But since Johnson had an innate ability to read people, he would adapt this technique to individuals who he was trying to persuade. A lot of great civil rights

---

[57] The Johnson Treatment, Dead Presidents, 2/24/2014.

legislation got passed that way; unfortunately so did a lot of ruinous Great Society welfare programs.

President Reagan, on the other hand, used his personal charm and his movie star status to persuade congressmen to support his agenda. During a crucial stage of the selling of the Kemp-Roth Tax Cuts legislation, Reagan invited 15 Democratic congressmen to Camp David where he served drinks and told funny stories about the good old days of Hollywood. The tax cuts eventually passed.

The incentives for a representative or a senator to support a return to the Moon will be many and varied. While one might wish that our elected representatives would make their decisions solely on what they perceive to be best for the country, that is an ideal more often than a reality. Some congressmen will have to be given other inducements in a manner that has been aptly compared, by Otto Bismarck, to sausage making.

The reason why NASA centers are spread out over the country is because Lyndon Johnson realized that members of Congress are motivated by baser things than mere patriotism. There is no reason that the Johnson Spaceflight Center is in Texas separate from the Kennedy Space Center in Florida except to make sure that the Florida and Texas congressional delegations are supporters of NASA funding. California, Ohio, and Alabama also have major NASA facilities for the same reason.

Sadly, too many congressmen are like the character in *The Godfather: Part II*, who just wants to "wet his beak" when it comes to NASA projects. They are more than willing to vote for a return to the Moon so long as it means contracts and jobs in their districts. These people have to be accommodated, since the solution arrived at by Vito Corleone is off the table.

If the carrot doesn't work, there is always the stick. An American president can do a lot of harm to a recalcitrant member of Congress if he has a mind to. Government contacts for a particular district can dry up just as much as they can manifest. A member of Congress who doesn't want to play ball may find him or herself without party support in the next election. He or she might even find a very appealing primary opponent to deal with should the president feel particularly put out.

The president always has the veto pen if a funding bill finds its way to his desk that doesn't give enough money to his priorities, such as a return to the Moon program. President George W. Bush offered his first veto threat when it looked as if the House was going to gut the Vision for Space Exploration. It turned out that he didn't have to; then House Majority Leader Tom DeLay, using his power to determine what does and does not get to the floor, made it known that the appropriations bill funding NASA would not be voted on until President Bush's space exploration program was fully funded. That illustrates one of the great principles of getting things done in the House, i.e., making powerful friends. It was too bad that DeLay was obliged to leave the House later to deal with trumped-up, politically-motivated ethics charges. In any case, DeLay would not have been majority leader for much longer, since the Democrats took over the House in 2006.

That last event illustrates another principle to bear in mind when shepherding a long-term program like a return to the Moon. All power, like glory, is fleeting.

Selling the Plan: Dealing with the Public

The National Research Council found[58] that while the
public has generally favorable views toward space
exploration and NASA, little support exists for increasing
spending on space efforts like a return to the Moon. Many
politicians have concluded that the political cost of urging
more spending, which a return to the Moon would require,
would be too high.

On the other hand, while there may be little support for
increased spending on space exploration, it is by no means
clear that there is significant opposition to it either. This
state of affairs suggests that an opportunity exists for an
American president to shape public opinion, to persuade
the American people that the benefits of returning to the
Moon make the cost worth it, that the costs are not all that
onerous, and that the costs of not going back to the Moon
would ultimately be heavier.

No one becomes President of the United States without a
certain degree of political and rhetorical skills which are
necessary to persuade people to vote for him/her. The same
skills can be brought to bear to sell a return to the Moon
program to the general public, going beyond making the
big speech.

One of the problems that have bedeviled past presidential
space initiatives has been the unwillingness of some
presidents, having started them, to publicly mention them
again. Kennedy made the famous Rice University speech
about the Moon race that has become even more famous
than the original speech before the joint session of

---

[58] Pathways to Exploration. Chapter 3: Public and Stakeholder
Attitudes, The National Academies Press, 2015.

Congress. The elder Bush, seeing his space exploration initiative flounder in Congress, tried to emulate Kennedy by making his own speech at Texas A & I University in Kingsville, Texas,[59] an odd choice for the subject, as it turned out. The younger Bush never mentioned the Vision for Space Exploration again, as if, having checked off the box, he was bored by his own initiative.

One of the secrets to selling something like a return to the Moon is to talk about it in a way that conveys enthusiasm for the project. That doesn't mean making a Rice University speech every month. But it does mean that it has to be mentioned in speeches along with other public policy initiatives. In this way, a return to the Moon is presented as being as ordinary as a tax reform package, a health care initiative, and anything else that is on the agenda. It would also be appropriate to make the speech concerning the return to the Moon initiative to appropriate audiences, such as student groups, industry associations, and so on.

Presidential surrogates are equally important for the task of selling the return to the Moon program. Along those lines, it is a good idea for the NASA Administrator to be willing and able to speak publicly and persuasively in support of it. Other presidential surrogates include: the vice president, friendly members of Congress, and the White House Science advisor.

Selling the return to the Moon should not be confined to the president and his surrogates and should include much more than making speeches. In the masterful book, *Marketing the Moon: The Selling of the Apollo Lunar Program*, authors

---

[59] Remarks at the Texas A&I University Commencement Ceremony in Kingsville. President George H. W. Bush, 5/11/1990.

David Meeran Scott and Richard Jurak describe how NASA undertook to sell the Moon program to the American people in the 1960s. For example, the main medium for selling Apollo and for including the American people in its operation was television. For a return to the Moon, the main medium will be the Internet and the social media tools it has to offer.

YouTube videos as well as tweets and Facebook posts from people involved in the project will go a long way toward selling a return to the Moon to the public and, more importantly, keeping it sold. The instant nature of social media also allows supporters of the project to immediately engage its opponents, countering their arguments, and making sure that the message that returning to the Moon is a good thing remains the theme.

The best way to present the story of the return to the Moon is to tell it as a narrative. The stories can be anything from an engineer who saw the first moon landing as a child and is now working on the next moon landing to young scientist eager to study the secrets that the Moon might have to offer. People identify with people more than with abstract ideas like the glory of exploration or the wonder of science. Enthusiasm, in this way, can be infectious.

Above all, when selling the return to the Moon program to the public, one has to be totally transparent. When problems arise, and they always do when one is undertaking such a huge project, it behooves anyone defending a return to the Moon to get out in front of them. Explain why the particular problem occurred, whether it is a cost overrun or an accident that kills astronauts. More importantly, one should explain how the problem is going to be fixed. Most people are understanding so long as they are told the truth in a forthright manner rather than finding out via back channels and rumors.

If the public is engaged sufficiently and as the benefits become more apparent, support for a return to the Moon will grow. The trick is to be persistent, truthful, and eloquent in presenting the arguments. No large-scale space project will sell itself. Do not presume, as other politicians have, that the "coolness factor" will make the virtues of a return to the Moon self-evident. To do that would be to suffer the fate of Newt Gingrich and his Moon base proposal. A politician can stand being called wrong; he or she is not doing the job right if this doesn't happen. But having a proposal called "zany" is certain death, both for the proposal and the politician. The goal is to make a return to the Moon a reality, not to have it become a national joke.

Selling the Plan: Dealing with the Media

At first glance, selling a return to the Moon plan to the media should be the easiest task of all. As skeptical and as cynical as many reporters pretend to be, they can become like wide-eyed children when they get to cover a space mission. This situation was true during the Apollo era, when Walter Cronkite melted down with awe and wonder when the pictures of the first men to walk on the Moon aired on hundreds of millions of TV screens across the planet. It is true, for the most part, 45-plus years later, as the recent encounter with Pluto by the New Horizons probe proves.

Make sure that NASA and contractor people are available to the media. They should be prepped on how to answer questions in order to cast the return to the Moon program in the best light. While most in the mainstream media will be behind the program, some will feel obligated to ask tough questions out of professional obligation or, in some cases, professional snark. Make sure that good answers have been prepared.

One good idea would be to embed some reporters with various engineering and research teams at NASA and the commercial partners. A couple of reporters who have some science and/or engineering training should be embedded with astronaut crews while in training. Consider having a reporter actually be part of a crew that goes to the Moon on an early mission.

One study done of embedded reporters during the Iraq War suggested that they tended to identify with the soldiers they accompanied[60] and tended to write more positive stories.

---

[60] Embedded Verses Unilateral Perspectives on the Iraq War, Shaharia

Some news organizations considered this to be a bug. The military, which was stung by what it considered overly negative coverage during the Vietnam War, considered it to be a feature. NASA would garner similar benefits.

In recent years an entirely new branch of journalism has grown up outside the newspaper/television/radio/magazine axis. Everyone with a computer and an Internet connection can now be a journalist, their success only limited by the number of page views they can garner. This development has served to democratize journalism and punditry to some extent. The results have been somewhat mixed.

In space journalism, some well-informed and insightful bloggers exist who are familiar with the various issues involving space policy. However, others tend to use their Internet connections to rant about their personal issues. The latter type tend to be negative, cantankerous, and often more than a little boring.

The main issues that drive what may be called "the Internet Rocketeer Club," concern how the civil space program is run. Public debate about the course of the civil space program is a welcome thing in a democracy. However, very often, more heat than light can be generated with *ad hominem* attacks, accusations of bad faith, and the venting of conspiracy theories. Avoid these people as if they were Ebola. Nothing you can say, no facts you can present, no appeals to either reason or passion will convince them of the error of their ways.

Fahmy and Thomas J. Johnson, Newspaper Research Journal, Summer 2007.

Treat the more intelligent space bloggers as the equals of their more conventional counterparts in the mainstream media. Set up interviews for them with astronauts, engineers, and top NASA managers. They will be flattered by the attention and will be more likely to create favorable posts.

When things go wrong, and they will go wrong, be as entirely open as possible. The tendency in any large organization is to try to conceal mistakes. Good reporters can smell this out as if it were rotten fish. Lay out why the mistake happened, and give a good account of how the mistake is going to be rectified. Most reporters will be appreciative of the honesty and will cut the program a break.

Selling the Plan: The International Partners

A return to the Moon is going to be an American led and an international effort. Cost sharing issues aside, the diplomatic advantages of including allies are too profound not to take on international partners. It goes without saying that such an effort is going to require some adroit diplomacy.

One great and successful example exists of a successful international space project. When President Reagan first announced the project that eventually became the International Space Station, Canada, the European Union, and Japan were invited to join as partners. Later, when President Bill Clinton restructured the space station program, he brought Russia on as a major partner. This act more than any other ended the political controversy surrounding the space station project and effectively ended attempts to defund it in Congress.

It goes without saying that American allies should be given preference in choosing which countries to select as partners in the return to the moon effort. Canada, Japan, and the European Union, the original partners in the space station project, are natural choices. India and South Korea should also be invited to the effort, since they are emerging technology powers and American allies.

Russia and China are also possible candidates for partners in a return to the Moon effort. Russia has been a partner in the International Space Station project since the early 1990s. China is a rising space power, with several crewed flights having been completed as well as several lunar probes, including the Chang'e 3 lunar lander and Yutu rover.

On the other hand, two things argue against including Russia or China as partners in the return to the Moon effort. First, the regimes running both countries are enthusiastic human rights abusers. No one would contemplate, for example, taking on Iran or North Korea as partners in any enterprise, not to speak of something as high profile and as important as going back to the Moon. Second, both countries harbor imperialist ambitions to the detriment of some other partners likely to be involved in the return to the Moon effort. The embarrassment would be acute if, in the middle of a lunar effort, China and Japan were to go to war over the East China Sea or Russia and the European Union, along with the United States and Canada, were to start fighting over Poland or the Baltic States.

Nevertheless, the possibility of joining the return to the Moon effort should be dangled in front of nations like China and Russia as incentives for good behavior on Earth. If China were to sign an agreement with Japan concerning the disputed East China Sea and if it moved to improve its human rights record, it should be considered for partnership. Similarly, if Russia were to respect the sovereignty of its neighbors, such as the Ukraine, and improve its treatment of dissidents, it too could be considered for full membership in the return to the Moon enterprise.

Finally, the State of Israel should be considered for partnership in the effort. On paper, Israel would make an excellent partner. It is a democracy and a firm American ally. Moreover, Israel is a technologically advanced society; it has launched satellites, both military and scientific, on its own launch vehicles. Israeli experiments have flown on the space shuttle. An Israeli astronaut, Ilan

Ramon, died on the space shuttle *Columbia* and is considered a national hero. Moreover, Israel is already cooperating in research of the Moon, being a member of the NASA Center for Moon Research. A private Israeli team, SpaceIL is a contestant in the Google Lunar XPrize.

Including Israel in the return to the Moon partnership has a downside. The move might cause conflict with other partners, especially in Europe, with large Muslim populations and governments that have become increasingly hostile to the Jewish state. The United States may, at the last extremis, be called upon to choose between some European countries and Israel. While realpolitik would suggest excluding Israel as the price of European participation, a strict adherence to American values dictates including the Jewish state and letting the Europeans decide whether or not to boycott the return to the Moon effort based on Israeli participation.

Designing a return to the Moon with international participation helps to share costs and to access technological expertise outside the United States. The arrangement also serves as an expression of soft power. International participation enhances American leadership in space, binding allied countries closer to the United States in a common, mutually beneficial endeavor. Moreover, a return to the Moon provides an incentive for certain countries like Russia and China to adhere to international norms in foreign policy and human rights, the better to join in the greatest adventure of all.

Selling the Plan: The Private Sector

In the old days of the Apollo program, attracting the private sector to a large-scale space project was easy. NASA doled out lots of money for companies like Boeing and Lockheed to build the hardware to take men to the Moon and return them safely to the Earth. No company in its right mind would fail to bid for such contracts if it had a chance of winning them.

A new model for how NASA interacts with the private sector was developed in the wake of President George W. Bush's Vision for Space Exploration. The Commercial Orbital Transportation System program charged private companies to compete for first resupply and then crew transfer services for the International Space Station. President Obama later doubled down on the crewed version of the approach with the Commercial Crew program.

The COTS model suggests that including the private sector, not just as contractors, but as partners in a return to the Moon effort would be a viable option. The first part of a return to the Moon to which the model could be applied is the lunar lander. Just as with the two commercial crew vehicles, NASA would start a competition to build a commercial lunar lander, chipping in a little bit of money for the chosen competitors, winnowing them down with each round until at least two vendors are picked. Likely a number of lunar landers, ranging from small ones that could deliver rovers and other packages to larger ones that would deliver crewed modules and habitats to the lunar surface, will be developed.

For longer stays, some kind of habitat or collection of habitats would be needed. A company called Bigelow

Aerospace, using a technology pioneered by NASA, has developed inflatable habitats that can be used either as part of a space station or as a lunar base. One of these modules has already been attached to the International Space Station. The company envisions a commerce space station made of one or more of these modules that customers, including NASA, could lease. The commercial space station is envisioned as a follow up to the ISS when it finally ends its useful life in 2024.

Private companies, large and small, would likely line up to become commercial partners in a return to the Moon effort. If they are confident that the return to the Moon will actually happen and will not succumb to the curious political attention deficit disorder that has afflicted so many other large-scale space projects, private businesses will be eager to participate, not only for the possibility of making money, but for the glory of participating in a world historical project. Many space entrepreneurs grew up on stories of the Apollo program.

The main problem with using the commercial crew model for parts of the return to the Moon, such as the lunar lander and the moon base, is convincing Congress that it is viable. Congress has consistently underfunded the commercial crew program to build a privately operated space craft to take astronauts to and from the International Space Station. Anger at President Obama's abrupt cancellation of the Constellation program and skepticism that the government funded/commercially operated model is optimal has contributed to this behavior. The people who write the checks have to be brought on board Commercial Luna, as we might call it, before the return to the moon program gets under way. In particular, any temptation to single source any hardware obtained by the program has to be resisted. At least two vendors must be acquired and maintained for each major piece of hardware, especially a lunar lander, to make sure all needed items are available should a major failure occur in one vendor's product.

Sometime in the Near Future…

The wall-to-wall big-screen TV has been displaying talking heads on one half of the screen and an image of the Artemis lunar lander on the other half for the past hour. It is the first crewed spacecraft to set down on the lunar surface in 50 years. The old man watching the TV reflects that despite the passage of decades and the advance of technology, the need to fill air time during the high points of the flight of Orion 3 has not changed since the age of over-the-air broadcasting and analog televisions. The cable news network on which he has watched most of the mission has had a procession of celebrity scientists, former astronauts, politicians, and media pundits to discuss every aspect of the first flight to the Moon in decades.

The media is vastly different than it was when men first walked on the Moon 53 years before. Then only three major networks existed. Now, most televisions can access a broad range of news and science-oriented channels that can cover the return to the Moon from their own unique perspectives. That does not include the various ways that the Internet and social media cover the events.

With that in mind, the old man picks up his tablet and checks his social media feeds. The NASA and the Artemis Twitter accounts are abuzz, creating a minute-by-minute account of what is happening both on Earth and on the Moon. The old man adds his impressions of the event to his own channels and then adds a picture of his living room, filled with friends and family members. Three generations, only a handful of whom had seen men walk on the Moon in the 1960s and 70s, are munching snacks, playing with their own electronics, or just watching raptly what is happening on the Moon hundreds of thousands of miles away.

The crewed lander has been preceded by a cargo ship containing a rover, an inflatable habitat, and supplies weeks ago. The camera on the cargo lander is what shows the Artemis standing on the lunar surface. It tracks the lunar lander as it descends to the landing site on a tail of fire, on the north rim of the Shackleton Crater. That is something they never got to see 50-plus years ago.

Suddenly, the moderator on the news channel stops the banter with her guests and says, "We just got word that the EVA is about to begin. The mission commander is already in her moon suit and has entered the Artemis airlock."

The old man notices that some of the younger people are already putting on their VR googles. They will get a full 3D view of the first person to walk on the Moon in decades. The old man, however, is just old-fashioned enough to want to watch it on the flat screen.

The airlock door slides open, and a pair of space suited legs appears. The old man thinks it amusing that the commander of the Orion 3 is a female Air Force officer. Fifty years ago, female astronauts at NASA were nine years in the future, and Sally Ride's first flight was 14 years in the future. The commander of Orion 3 is fully qualified, having spent two tours on the International Space Station. But the old man thinks that her selection was a conscious decision by NASA to boast of how diverse the space agency is these days.

The space suit she wears is modern as well, a form-fitting costume that uses "active materials" to keep up the pressure on her body to compensate for the lack thereof on the lunar surface. She moves as gracefully as a gymnast, clambering down the ladder of the Artemis in easy steps. The old man smiles, remembering the bulky moon suits that the Apollo astronauts wore, making their movements awkward.

She stands at the bottom of the ladder and talks to Mission Control about the state of the Artemis on the lunar surface.

Then comes the great moment!

"I'm going to step down now."

She steps off lightly and plants both boots on the lunar surface.

"We have returned to the Moon in the spirit of peace and scientific exploration," the commander of the Artemis says, "and that was a heck of a leap for a woman."

As likely happens at hundreds of thousands of venues, from living rooms like this to a crowded Times Square, everyone present breaks out in spontaneous applause.

The old man has a tear on his cheek. One of the kids notices this. "Was it like this the first time, Grandpa?"

The old man smiles down at her. "This time's better. Because this time, we're going to stay."

Also by Mark R. Whittington:

Children of Apollo: The Space Race Gambit

Children of Apollo: The Hard Road to the Stars

Children of Apollo: The First Woman on the Moon

The Last Moonwalker and Other Stories

The Man from Mars: The Asteroid Mining Caper

Gabriella's War

Nocturne: A Novel of Suspense (with Chantal Whittington)